U0490997

Entrepreneur Kid
创业儿童

加布丽
发明的完美发夹

Gabby Invents the
Perfect Hair Bow

（汉英对照）

茹燕子（Erica Swallow）著
曾俐 绘/译

张欣 审校

中国财经出版传媒集团
经济科学出版社
Economic Science Press

图书在版编目(CIP)数据

加布丽发明的完美发夹: 汉英对照/(美)茹燕子(Erica Swallow)著; 曾俐译/绘.—北京: 经济科学出版社, 2018.12
(创业儿童)
ISBN 978-7-5141-9445-6

Ⅰ.①加… Ⅱ.①茹…②曾… Ⅲ.①创业-儿童读物-汉、英 Ⅳ.①F241.4-49

中国版本图书馆CIP数据核字(2018)第133382号

加布丽发明的完美发夹(汉英对照)

茹燕子(Erica Swallow) 著
曾 俐 绘/译

责任编辑: 周国强
责任校对: 杨晓莹
责任印制: 邱 天

经济科学出版社出版、发行 新华书店经销

社址: 北京市海淀区阜成路甲28号 邮编: 100142
电话: 总编部 010-88191217 发行部 010-88191522
网址: www.esp.com.cn
邮箱: esp@esp.com.cn
网店: 经济科学出版社旗舰店(天猫)
网址: http://jjkxcbs.tmall.com
印刷: 中煤(北京)印务有限公司
开本: 889×1194 20开 2印张 30000字
版次: 2018年12月第1版 2018年12月第1次印刷
书号: ISBN 978-7-5141-9445-6
定价: 48.00元

(图书出现印装问题, 本社负责调换。电话: 010-88191510)
(版权所有 侵权必究 打击盗版 举报热线: 010-88191661
QQ:2242791300 营销中心电话:010-88191537
电子邮箱: dbts@esp.com.cn)

加布丽·古德温喜欢跳舞,她从三岁就开始上舞蹈课了!

Gabby Goodwin loves to dance. She's been taking lessons since she was three years old!

无论是在舞台或是去上学，她总是保持着靓丽的发型。

Whether she's on the stage or just heading to school, her hair is always just right.

从卷发到玉米辫，从辫子头到丸子头，她尤其喜欢挑出那些色彩缤纷的彩色发夹，来搭配她的发型！

From curls and cornrows to braids and buns, Gabby especially loves picking out colorful bows and barrettes to top off her hair styles!

"妈妈,我们今天戴粉的和红的发夹好吗?"加布丽坐下来梳头时问妈妈。

"当然好呀,只是希望你今天别再把发夹弄丢了。"妈妈说。

"Can we do pink and red today, Mommy?" Gabby asks as she sits down for her daily hairstyling.

"You got it! Let's hope you don't lose any bows today," her mother says.

无论加布丽在哪儿,她似乎总会弄丢发夹。

结果呢,今天也不例外。

No matter where Gabby is, she always seems to lose her hair bows.

As it turns out, this day would be no different.

古德温太太上班前，先把加布丽送到学校，然后把弟弟送到托儿所。

"祝你们拥有美好的一天！"她对兄妹俩说道。

Mrs. Goodwin dropped Gabby off for school and took her little brother to daycare before heading to work.

"Have a great day!" she told them both.

加布丽和古德温太太组成了出色的团队。加布丽负责设计发夹样式和挑选颜色，并给每个产品取名字。同时，她还掌管公司财务，确保产品库存，主导活动中的销售。

有顾客在网上购买发夹时，加布丽还会寄出一张手写的感谢卡。

Gabby and her mom make a great team. Gabby chooses bow designs and colors and names all of the products. She also handles the company's money, makes sure they have enough products, and leads sales at events.

When customers order bows online, she sends each of them a handwritten thank you card, too.

尽管历经了数年时间，但加布丽的公司终于变成了现实。

如今，加布丽将成千上万的发夹卖给了美国各州和世界各地的孩子和家长们，免除了他们丢失发夹的烦恼。她还因此登上了全国的电视和广播！

It took a few years, but Gabby's company is finally a reality.

Today, she has sold thousands of bows to kids and parents in every American state and all over the world who were tired of losing their barrettes. She's also been on national TV and radio!

琢磨出想做什么样的发夹之后,她们请教堂的一位朋友帮忙把设计构想画了出来,这样就能展示给大家看了。这位朋友是一位很出色的画家,他答应了要帮这个忙。

After figuring out the type of barrette they wanted to make, they asked a friend from church to help them draw their idea, so they could share it with others. He was a really good artist and agreed to help out.

"加布丽，你觉得怎样才能让发夹卡在你的头发上呢？"古德温太太问道。

加布丽说，在发扣周围得有坚固耐用的发夹齿。她们还认为发夹应该有两面，这样大家就总能看到有趣的设计。

"奶奶很讨厌我夹反的发夹！"加布丽说。

加布丽和妈妈联合起来，开始着手设计她们能想到的最棒的发夹！

"What do you think makes a bow stay in your hair, Gabby?" Mrs. Goodwin asked.

Gabby said they needed strong teeth. They also thought barrettes should have two faces, so people could always see the fun designs.

"Grandma hates when my bows flip the wrong way!" Gabby said.

The duo was off to work, designing the best hair barrette they could imagine!

类似问题持续不断。

直到有一天,加布丽说:"妈妈,今天是不是一个设计发夹的好日子呢?"

古德温太太无法拒绝。她俩坐到餐桌前,开动起了脑筋。

The questions never ended.

"Mommy, wouldn't today be a great day to design a bow?" Gabby said one day.

Mrs. Goodwin couldn't say no. The two sat at the kitchen table and brainstormed.

俩人在超市购物时，她问："妈妈，商店会卖我的新发夹吗？"

"Mommy, will my bows be sold in stores?" she asked while the two were out grocery shopping.

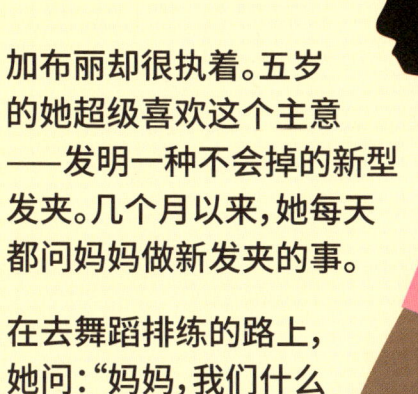

加布丽却很执着。五岁的她超级喜欢这个主意——发明一种不会掉的新型发夹。几个月以来，她每天都问妈妈做新发夹的事。

在去舞蹈排练的路上，她问："妈妈，我们什么时候自己做新发夹？"

Gabby was persistent. She was five years old and loved the idea of making a new type of bow that wouldn't fall out. She asked her mom about the bow idea every day for months.

"Mommy, when will we make my bow?" she asked on the way to dance rehearsal.

一天早上，古德温太太正给加布丽编着头发，她抱怨道："我不知道为什么还给你弄头发，你每天回家这些发夹都会少一半。"

"妈妈，我们要自己做发夹吗？"加布丽兴奋地问。

"不，不，不。我只是在想有些人应该去做新的发夹。"古德温太太一边回答，一边把最后一个发夹别在加布丽的头发上。

One morning, while styling Gabby's hair, Mrs. Goodwin huffed, "I don't even know why I'm doing your hair. Half of these bows are going to be gone when you get home."

"Mommy! Are we going to make a bow?" Gabby shouted excitedly.

"No, no, no. I was just thinking that somebody should make a bow," Mrs. Goodwin replied, placing the final barrette in Gabby's hair.

时间飞逝，古德温太太一直琢磨着牧师说的话。她也想解决问题，但是，谁来做这些神奇发夹呢？

Days and weeks went on. Mrs. Goodwin could not stop thinking about what the pastor had said. She wanted the problem fixed, but who was going to make these magical bows?

接着，家庭牧师贝利也发来一则消息。

他建议古德温太太自己做发夹。"听起来像是你应该打入发夹市场了。"他写道。

古德温太太苦笑："但是，我实在太忙了！"

"听起来像是你应该打入发夹市场了。"
"Sounds like a market you need to break into."

Then, a message from the family's pastor popped up.

Pastor Bailey suggested that she make a new bow. "Sounds like a market you need to break into," he wrote.

Mrs. Goodwin scoffed, "But I'm so busy!"

"我受不了这些发夹!"
"I can't stand those barrettes!"

"我根本不用发夹了。"
"I don't even use them anymore."

"我拿橡皮筋固定它们。"
"I twist a rubber band around them to make them stay."

...

"如果你发现好用的,也请告诉我一声。"
"When you find some that work, let me know."

古德温太太拿起手机在网上抱怨道:"简直难以置信!我女儿头上的发夹又少了一半!到底有没有好用的发夹?"

各处的妈妈们纷纷回复了她。

Mrs. Goodwin picked up her phone and posted a rant online: "I can't believe it! Half of my daughter's bows are gone again! Are there any barrettes out there that actually work?"

Mothers from all around replied to Mrs. Goodwin's message.

回到家，加布丽和弟弟写起了作业。

古德温太太垂头丧气地把新买来的发夹按颜色区分开来。因为发夹总是弄丢得太快，家里每两周就得买新的。

Back at home, Gabby and her little brother started their homework.

Mrs. Goodwin was frustrated as she separated the latest purchase of Gabby's hair bows by color. The family had to buy bows every two weeks, because they fell out so often.

午餐时间，加布丽的老师给全体学生家长发了一张孩子们在艺术课上画画的照片。

看到照片，古德温太太叹息道："天啊！加布丽的头发看起来糟透了！"加布丽头上的发夹少了一半，头发凌乱地披散着。

"发夹都跑哪里去了？"古德温太太心烦意乱，得想个办法让发夹不再掉下来。

Around lunchtime, Gabby's teacher sent a photo to all of her students' parents of the kids drawing pictures in art class.

Mrs. Goodwin gasped, "Ahhh! Gabby's hair looks horrible!" Half of Gabby's barrettes were missing, and her hair was all over the place!

"Where do all of her bows go?" she thought, frantically. There had to be a way to keep the bows from falling out.

古德温太太确保公司运作正常，负责与其他公司合作，制作并出售她们一起设计的双面发夹。

加布丽说，等她长大以后也希望可以和她的女儿继续经营发夹公司，就像现在的自己和妈妈一样。

Mrs. Goodwin makes sure the business is running by partnering with other companies to manufacture and sell the bows the two designed together.

Gabby says when she grows up she wants to run her bow business with her daughter just like she and her mommy do now.

加布丽的全家都以实际行动支持着她。她爸爸是一个喜剧演员,他有丰富的舞台经验,能帮助加布丽做演讲训练。曾经开口就紧张的她,现在已敢于在任何人面前侃侃而谈!

Gabby's whole family helps out with work. Her daddy is a comedian and helps her practice for speeches, since he has so much experience talking on stages. She used to get nervous, but now she can speak in front of anyone!

连加布丽的弟弟都来帮忙了——尤其是当公司订单太多的时候,加布丽就办"打包派对"。她超级需要帮忙,因为业务量巨大,她自己完全忙不过来!

Even Gabby's little brother helps out — especially when Gabby throws packing parties for the days when her company gets a lot of orders. She needs tons of help when there are too many orders to handle alone!

创业艰难百战多。不是所有人都想买她的发夹，有时，商店也没地方存放货品。被拒绝是残酷的，但加布丽已然学会了面对。

Starting a business is hard. Not everyone wants to buy her bows. Sometimes stores don't have space to carry them either. Hearing "no" is tough, but she has learned how to deal with it.

上学、跳舞、开公司，这一切让加布丽忙得不亦乐乎。有时她不得不放弃生日派对和娱乐，因为她要确保发夹准时发货。顾客们都盼望着呢！

Having school, dance, and a business makes for a busy life, too. Gabby has to miss birthday parties and playtime sometimes, so she can make sure bow orders are mailed on time. Customers are counting on her!

加布丽热爱她的事业。她喜欢用自己最完美的发夹来帮助小女孩们一整天都保持着可爱的发型。

如今，加布丽在全世界做演讲，讲述她开公司的经历。无论是讲给大人还是小孩听，她都鼓励大家要有一个大大的梦想。

Gabby loves her business, though. She loves that she helps little girls keep their hair cute all day with the best hair bow ever.

These days, Gabby gives speeches all around the world, talking about her experience starting a company. Whether she's speaking to children or adults, she always encourages them to dream big.

"信，则成。"加布丽说道，"为所能为，永不放弃。"

现在轮到你了……你想为这个世界解决什么问题呢？

"If you believe, you can achieve," Gabby says. "Try your best, work hard, and never give up."

Now it's your turn... What problems do you want to solve in the world?

作者寄语

《加布丽发明的完美发夹》讲述的是7岁的加布丽·古德温与妈妈罗瑟琳·古德温以加布丽发夹公司的名义发明并获得新型发夹专利的故事。

加布丽发夹公司的故事始于2011年南卡罗来纳州的哥伦比亚市,起因是古德温太太在社交媒体网站推特上抱怨时下设计的发夹不够人性化,说有些连卡口都没有,5岁女儿的头发都绑不住。这一推文,获得了古德温太太社交网络中父母们的一致赞同,这一情形在本书中有非常形象生动的描绘。不论远近,都有妈妈们说自己也遇到同样的问题。然而,古德温太太始终没法抗拒古德温家族牧师的回应。

"听上去倒像是值得打入的市场。"赫伯特·贝利牧师在推特上回复说。

古德温太太和先生麦克·古德温早在为人父母之前就一直去贝利博士的教堂做礼拜。贝利博士见证了麦克从大学辅导员到喜剧行业老少咸宜的"谐星"这一职业转变。贝利博士还亲历了古德温太太在医疗保健政策方面的职业成长,以及她的两个孩子——加布丽和弟弟麦克尔的出生。可以说,在相当长一段时期内,古德温夫妇都将贝利博士看作是他们人生的关键影响者。

故事还在继续……此事搁浅数月后,古德温太太在给女儿梳头时偶然提及对发夹的不满之情。5岁的加布丽第一反应是问妈妈要不要一起做一个新发夹。虽然每次古德温太太都试着避开这个话题,加布丽却

加布丽·古德温在学校卖发夹。摄影:安德斯·克罗克,雷内摄影
(Andris Kinloch, A. Renee Photography)

总是问个不停，直到有一天，母女二人坐在餐桌旁开始筹划此事。

2014年，在加布丽7岁的时候，"加布丽发夹"正式投入市场，如今它已成为一个国际品牌。截至2017年夏，加布丽发夹已经销往全美50个州以及全世界8个国家。发夹在网店以及"曾经的孩子"等实体零售店有售。在写作本书时，加布丽发夹共有三种蝴蝶结样式，设计灵感来自于父母对自儿女们的昵称：甜豌豆、小淑女、爸爸的甜心。很应景的是，"爸爸的甜心"这一款设计成了领结的样子，用以纪念加布丽爸爸在她生命中的影响。

加布丽发夹公司以及CEO加布丽·古德温因取得的巨大成功获奖无数，包括：南卡罗来纳州2015年度青年企业家，2016年企业可持续发展（以下简称SCORE）和山姆俱乐部小型企业竞赛冠军，2015年小型企业管理创意女性商业竞赛全国决赛选手，以及SCORE 2016年年度杰出多元公司。

加布丽和母亲在全国各地举行演讲，鼓励其他孩子拥有伟大梦想。我和插画师曾俐、摄影师丹·东贝在写这部书的时候拜访了加布丽一家。本书故事和图片取材于与加布丽及其家人的面谈及网上访谈。想要了解更多关于加布丽和她公司的故事，请访问网站：entrepreneurkid.com 和 gabbybows.com，里面有详细的视频、图片和其他信息。

罗瑟琳，加布丽·古德温和加布丽发卡公司。
摄影：安德斯·克罗克，雷内摄影 (Andris Kinloch, A. Renee Photography)

古德温一家　摄影：图人摄影 (People Photography)

你读过多少《创业儿童》的丛书？

《创业儿童》系列丛书共有四本书。通读全四册，了解其他孩子是如何开始创业的。通过解决生活中的问题，你也可以成为创业儿童。

How many Entrepreneur Kid books have you read?

There are four books in the Entrepreneur Kid series. Read them all to learn how other kids like you started their own businesses. You, too, can be an Entrepreneur Kid by solving problems around you.

扫码关注创作者

大开眼界

动物如何观察和适应世界

［加拿大］弗朗索瓦丝·维尔佩 著

燕子 译

中国科学技术出版社

·北 京·